Life in the Past

Victorian Toys

Mandy Ross

Heinemann
LIBRARY

www.heinemann.co.uk/library
Visit our website to find out more information about **Heinemann Library** books.

To order:

☎ Phone ++44 (0)1865 888066

▤ Send a fax to ++44 (0)1865 314091

💻 Visit the Heinemann Bookshop at *www.heinemann.co.uk/library* to browse our catalogue and order online.

First published in Great Britain by Heinemann Library, Halley Court, Jordan Hill, Oxford OX2 8EJ, part of Harcourt Education. Heinemann is a registered trademark of Harcourt Education Ltd.

Editorial: Lucy Thunder and Helen Cannons
Design: Ron Kamen and Paul Davies
Picture Research: Rebecca Sodergren and Liz Savery
Production: Edward Moore
Originated by Repro Multi-Warna
Printed and bound in Hong Kong and China by South China Printing Company
The paper used to print this book comes from sustainable resources.

ISBN 0 431 12142 7
08 07 06 05 04
10 9 8 7 6 5 4 3 2 1

British Library Cataloguing in Publication Data
Ross, Mandy
Victorian toys. – (Life in the past)
790.1'33'0941'09034

A full catalogue record for this book is available from the British Library.

Acknowledgements
The Publishers are grateful to the following for permission to reproduce photographs: Art Archive p**13**; Bridgeman Art Library pp**23**, **25**; Bridgeman Art Library/RSA, London p**4**; Bridgeman Art Library/Walker Galleries, Harrogate p**26**; Corbis/Bettmann p**14**; Fine Art Photographic Library Ltd/(by courtesy of N. R. Omell Gallery, London) p**6**; Hulton Archive pp**20**, **22**, **24**, **27**; Mary Evans Picture Library pp**8**, **18**; National Trust Photographic Library p**21**, **27**; Robert Opie pp**9**, **11**, **12**, **15**, **16**, **17**, **19**; Topham Picturepoint pp**5**, **7**, **10**, **28**.

Cover photo of a group of children playing marbles, c.1855, reproduced with permission of Hulton Archive.

Our thanks to Jane Shuter for her assistance in the preparation of this book.

Every effort has been made to contact copyright holders of any material reproduced in this book. Any omissions will be rectified in subsequent printings if notice is given to the Publishers.

Disclaimer
All the Internet addresses (URLs) given in this book were valid at the time of going to press. However, due to the dynamic nature of the Internet, some addresses may have changed, or sites may have ceased to exist since publication. While the author and publishers regret any inconvenience this may cause readers, no responsibility for any such changes can be excepted by either the author or the Publishers.

Contents

Who were the Victorians? 4

Toys then and now 6

Toys for the boys 8

Dolls for the girls 10

Books and comics 12

Printed treasures 14

What shall we play? 16

Skipping and string 18

Made or found 20

Too poor to play? 22

Outdoor sports 24

Free to roam 26

Let's find out! 28

Timeline 30

Glossary 31

Find out more 31

Index 32

Words written in bold, **like this**, are explained
in the Glossary.

Who were the Victorians?

Queen Victoria **reigned** in Britain from 1837 to 1901. People who lived during this time are called Victorians. Their lives were very different from ours today.

Queen Victoria

This painting from 1864 shows Queen Victoria with some of her nine children. ☞

For rich Victorians, life was very comfortable. But many Victorians were very poor indeed. Some could not afford to send their children to school, or to buy them toys or even shoes.

These Victorian children are playing in the street. Two of them do not have shoes.

Toys then and now

Toys were more expensive in Victorian times. Even rich children had fewer toys than children today. Many children from poor families had no toys at all. They played outdoors instead.

These children are playing outdoors with soap bubbles and a broom. ☞

Most Victorian toys were made out
of **natural materials**, such as
wood, clay or cloth. Plastic,
electricity and computers
had not yet been
invented in
Victorian times.

Today many toys
are made out of
plastic, like these
computer pets. ☞

Toys for the boys

Children from rich families had the most toys. Boys often had rocking horses, puppets, skittles and spinning tops. As the railways grew, toy trains became popular, too.

This boy rides on his wooden rocking horse.

👉 A fine set of Victorian toy
soldiers dressed in Scottish kilts.

Many boys played with toy soldiers
made out of lead, wood or tin. In
wealthy homes, children played on
their own in their playroom. Their
parents did not play with them often.

Dolls for the girls

Girls from rich families had dolls made out of cloth, with faces and hands made of wax or **porcelain**. They were expensive and easily broken. Girls had to play with them gently.

Noah's Ark animals

bubble pipes

animal skittles

Mr Punch

☞ This fine collection of toys might have belonged to a rich girl.

Doll's houses were very popular. They were built to copy grand houses. They had very detailed, tiny furniture. Girls in wealthy families were expected to play quietly and always be **ladylike**.

This grand doll's house has three floors.

Books and comics

Children's books were expensive so even rich families only had a few. Many children's books told Bible stories or **moral** tales. Some Victorian stories are still read today.

This story-book cover shows a mother reading aloud to her children. ☞

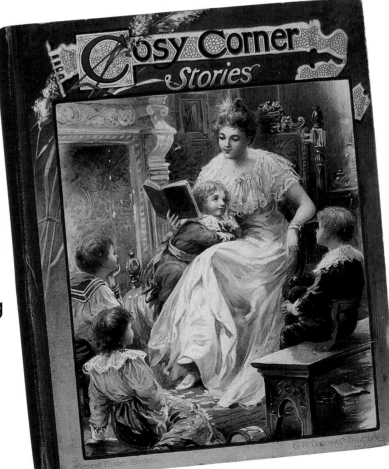

The *Halfpenny Comic* cost just half a penny to buy.

Comics were much cheaper than books. But children in the poorest families still could not afford them. In any case, they might not get enough schooling to learn to read.

Printed treasures

'Scraps' were printed paper pictures to collect and cut out. Collecting scraps was a popular Victorian **pastime** in families where there was a little money to spare.

☝ This is a Victorian cut-out doll with different outfits and hats. You see the front and back view of each costume.

☞ This Victorian scrapbook must have taken months or years to make.

Many Victorians enjoyed making scrapbooks. Some people collected scraps, postcards and printed pictures to glue into scrapbooks. Others pressed flowers or leaves.

What shall we play?

Children in **middle-class** families enjoyed playing with indoor toys, such as board games, dice, dominoes, cards and jigsaws. These were not too expensive.

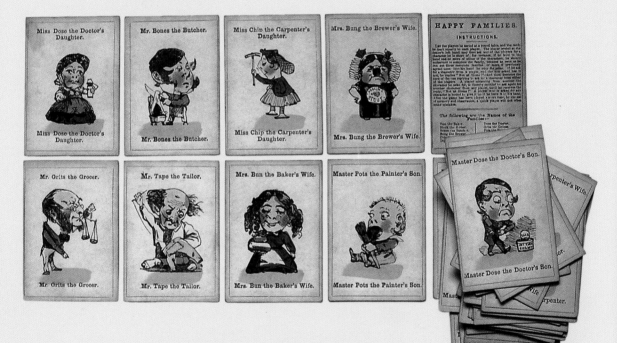

☞ A set of Victorian 'Happy Families' cards. This game is still played today.

☞ This beautiful toy Noah's Ark is carved out of wood and painted.

On Sundays in middle-class families, children were expected to read or play quietly. Some toys were based on the Bible. For instance, children might play with a toy Noah's Ark.

Many girls liked playing skipping games and cat's cradle, just as they do today. Girls from wealthier families had proper skipping ropes with carved wooden handles.

A Victorian photograph of a girl with her skipping rope.

Skipping was a cheap game for children from poorer families, too. They might use an old piece of washing line or rope.

This is part of an old skipping rhyme:

'He loves me,
he don't.
He'll have me,
he won't.
He would
if he could,
But he can't
so he don't.
A, B, C, D, E ...'

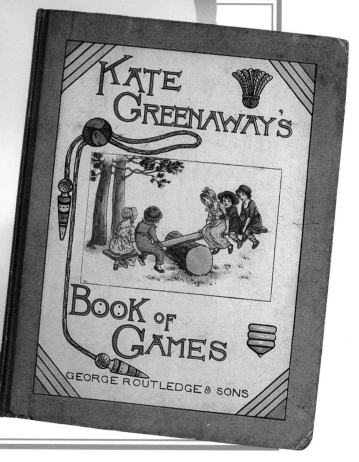

Made or found

Poorer Victorian children could buy cheap toys such as marbles and **jacks** for a penny or two. Or they played with any small things they could find, such as buttons, conkers or cherry stones.

Victorian children playing marbles out in the yard.

Home-made soft toys or rag dolls were made out of scraps of worn-out clothing or bedclothes. They were treasured. Teddy bears did not become popular until after Victorian times.

Soft toys of animals from the **British Empire** were popular with children.

Too poor to play?

Children from the poorest families had few toys. They often had little time to play, as many went to work from a young age. Some children worked at home, making things such as brushes.

👆 The poor children on the left are working to make dolls. The rich children are playing.

☞ These children are sailing a little home-made boat.

Poor children made their own toys out of household scraps, such as paper or wood. Kites were made out of paper and string. Boys might carve a wooden toy using a **pocket knife**.

Outdoor sports

Richer boys and girls played outdoor
ball games at home or at school.
Girls could not run fast in their long,
heavy dresses. They played **ladylike**
sports such as croquet or golf.

Croquet was played by
both boys and girls.

mallet

hoop

hockey stick   rugby ball

bike

cricket bat

A Victorian drawing of a shop selling all types of sports equipment.

Upper-class boys played outdoor sports at school, including rugby, cricket and hockey. It was important to be a good team player. Cycling was becoming popular, too.

Poor families' homes were very cramped. So poor children played outside, because there was nowhere else to play. Playing in the streets was much safer in Victorian times, because there were no cars.

Country children playing outside with a wheelbarrow.

👆 Ragged children playing
in the city streets.

Often, all the children in a street or
village played together, without adults
in charge. Many of their games are still
played today, such as hopscotch or tag.

Let's find out!

Life is very different for children today. But many toys and games have not changed. Which of your toys and games might a Victorian child recognize?

Children today skipping in a school playground.

You can find out more about popular Victorian toys and games at your local library or museum. Look out for displays of toys at Victorian houses that are open to the public.

 These Victorian toys are on display in the nursery of a big Victorian house.

Timeline

1837 Victoria is crowned Queen of Great Britain

1840 Clockwork toy trains are first made and sold. They are made out of tin.

1847 New **laws** reduce children's factory working hours to ten hours a day

1851 The Great Exhibition is held at the Crystal Palace, London. Many new toys are on display.

1854 British troops fight in the Crimean War against Russia

1861 Prince Albert, Victoria's husband, dies

1865 *Alice's Adventures in Wonderland*, by Lewis Carroll, is published

1870 Factories start making toy trains in Birmingham

1874 First edition of *Funny Folks*, a Victorian children's comic, is published

1883 *Treasure Island*, by Robert Louis Stevenson, is published

1891 Free schooling provided for all children

1901 Queen Victoria dies

Glossary

British Empire countries around the world under British control during Victoria's reign

jacks game where the player has to pick up several tiny objects while bouncing a small ball

ladylike well-mannered and polite

law rule made by parliament that everyone must obey

middle-class people who earn enough money to live comfortably, for instance doctors, lawyers and their families

moral to do with right and wrong

natural materials materials such as wood or cotton, not factory-made materials such as plastic or nylon

pastime hobby or game

pocket knife small folding knife or penknife

porcelain fine white clay or pottery

reign to rule as king or queen, or the period of time that a ruler is on the throne

upper-class people whose families are very rich or powerful

Find out more

More books to read

Look Inside a Victorian Toyshop, Brian Moses and Adam Hook (Wayland, 1997)

Life in Victorian Times: Sport and Leisure, Neil Morris (Belitha Press, 2000)

Life in Victorian Britain: The Victorians at Play, Rosemary Rees, (Heinemann Library, 1995)

Places and websites to visit

www.clanhouse.com
Here there are lots of useful links about the history of toys and children's books.

www.heinemannexplore.co.uk
The Heinemann Explore history website.

www.museumofchildhood.org.uk
The Museum of Childhood, London, has displays about Victorian toys and many aspects of Victorian childhood.

Index

ball games 24
Bible 12, 17
board games 16
books 12, 30
boys 8–9

comics 13, 30
croquet 24
cycling 25

dolls 10, 14, 21, 22
doll's houses 11

girls 10–11, 18, 24

home-made toys 21,
    23

jacks 20

kites 23

marbles 20
middle-class families
    16, 17

natural materials 7
Noah's Ark 10, 17

outdoor play 5, 6,
    24–7

playrooms 9
poor children 5, 6, 13,
    19, 20, 22-3, 26–7

rag dolls 21
rhymes 19
rich children 5, 8, 9,
    10, 12, 18, 24, 25
rocking horses 8

scraps and scrapbooks
    14, 15
skipping 18, 19, 28
soft toys 21
sports 24, 25
Sundays 17

teddy bears 21
toy soldiers 9

Victoria, Queen 4, 30
Victorians 4–5

work 22, 30